For my little niece Lizzy, who quite
rightly loves unicorns – H.W.

For my wife, Sol . . . she is
my unicorn – E.M.

First published in Great Britain 2023 by Red Shed, part of Farshore
An imprint of HarperCollins*Publishers*
1 London Bridge Street, London SE1 9GF
www.farshore.co.uk

HarperCollins*Publishers*
Macken House, 39/40 Mayor Street Upper,
Dublin 1, D01 C9W8

Copyright © HarperCollins*Publishers* Limited 2023
Written by Hannah Wilson
Illustrations by Emiliano Migliardo

ISBN 978 0 00 860354 0
001
Printed and bound in the UK using 100% Renewable Electricity at CPI Group (UK) Ltd.

A CIP catalogue record for this title is available from the British Library.

Stay safe online. Any website addresses listed in this book are correct at the time of going to print.
However, Farshore is not responsible for content hosted by third parties. Please be aware that
online content can be subject to change and websites can contain content that is unsuitable for
children. We advise that all children are supervised when using the internet.

MIX
Paper from
responsible sources
FSC™ C007454

This book is produced from independently certified FSC™ paper
to ensure responsible forest management.

For more information visit: www.harpercollins.co.uk/green

UNICORN WOULD Y♥U RATHER?

Written by Hannah Wilson
Illustrations by Emiliano Migliardo

RED SHED

Everybody loves unicorns! What's not to love about a beautiful horse with a spiralling horn and magical powers!

Do you like imagining silly situations and making wacky choices?

Do you love telling (uni)corny jokes?

Want to impress your friends with some weird and wonderful facts?

Read on for a sparkling selection of funny Would You Rather questions, hilarious jokes and fascinating unicorn facts . . .

Would you rather be a **unicorn**, with one horn...

OR a **two-nicorn**, with **two horns?**

The word 'unicorn' comes from the Latin words 'unus' (one) and 'cornu' (horn). A unicorn horn is called an alicorn.

Would you rather have a unicorn's **horsey head** . . .

OR its swishy tail?

In March 2022, 334 people in West Virginia, USA, set the record for the largest gathering of people wearing unicorn horns!

Would you rather have a **pet unicorn** to look after . . .

OR be a **unicorn's pet** yourself?

Would you rather meet a unicorn that can turn **invisible** . . . OR a glow-in-the-dark unicorn?

Would you rather give a unicorn a **bath** every day for **a year** . . .

OR scoop up a unicorn's **poop** for **a month?**

Would you rather go to a unicorn's **sleepover in the forest...**

OR invite a unicorn to a **sleepover at your house?**

Would you rather **unicorns were real,** and **elephants imaginary** . . .

OR **elephants real,** and **unicorns imaginary?**

A unicorn is an imaginary creature, like a mermaid or dragon. Stories about one-horned white horses became popular in medieval times (the period of European history from the 5th to 15th century CE), but some people believe ancient cave paintings also show unicorns!

Would you rather be
a **fire unicorn** . . .

OR a **snow unicorn?**

Would you rather be a **water** unicorn...

OR a **wind** unicorn?

Would you rather swim across a river full of unicrocs . . .

OR in a sea full of unisharks?

Unisharks aren't real – but a narwhal is a real-life Arctic mammal with a 3m-long tooth on its head. A sea unicorn!

Would you rather bounce on a trampoline with a unicorn . . .

OR go dancing at a unicorn disco?

Would you rather a **unicorn** cooked you dinner . . .

OR a **narwhal** cooked you breakfast?

Would you rather race a
unicorn with **eight legs** OR
be paired up with a unicorn in a
three-legged race?

The mysterious 'unicorn tarantula'
from Angola in Africa has a long, soft
horn on its back. Scientists have
no idea what it's for!

Would you rather meet a zebracorn OR a tigercorn?

Would you rather be **covered in sparkles** . . .

OR wear all the colours of the rainbow?

UNICORN JOKES!

Which unicorn has a cold?
The achoo-nicorn.

Which unicorn smells?
The poo-nicorn.

Where do unicorns throw their rubbish?
In the glitter bin.

**What do unicorns
say when they kiss?**
Ouch!

**What do you call a unicorn
without a horn?**
Pointless.

Knock knock.
Who's there?
U.
U who?
U-nicorn.

Would you rather burp unicorn-shaped bubbles . . .

BURP!

OR fart rainbows?

Would you rather ride a
super-speedy unicorn with magic
hooves that can run extra fast . . .

OR be able to ride on
a magical winged unicorn?

A pegacorn is a mythical flying
unicorn, inspired by Pegasus, a
winged horse from Greek legend.

Would you rather see a unicorn climb like a gecko . . .

OR hop like a rabbit?

Hopping from the pages of medieval Arabic stories is Almiraj, a mythical golden one-horned rabbit so terrifying that wild beasts fled at the sight of it!

Would you rather be a pirate who has **dug up buried treasure**...

OR a daring explorer who has
discovered a unicorn?

In about 1292, Italian explorer Marco Polo discovered unicorns in Sumatra (now part of Indonesia). They were actually rhinoceroses, of course!

Would you rather have a **scaly snakeicorn** as a pet . . .

OR a **woolly sheepicorn?**

In 2019, a sheep was born in Australia with just one horn growing from the centre of its forehead. Joey the 'unicorn sheep' was whisked away from the farm and looked after as a family pet!

Would you rather ride to school on a **unicorn** . . .

OR on a **dragon?**

The mythical Qilin, sometimes known as the Chinese unicorn, has a single horn on a dragon's head and flames wrapping around its scaly body.

Would you rather be a **daytime** unicorn relaxing in the sunshine . . .

OR a **nocturnal** unicorn galloping in the moonlight?

Would you rather be able to **heal wounds . . .**

OR be **super strong?**

Would you rather
share your house with
a giant unicorn . . .

OR have ten tiny unicorns living in your hair?

Would you rather have a **table tennis contest** with a unicorn . . .

OR challenge one to a **dance off?**

Would you rather be able to read people's minds . . .

OR move things with your mind?

UNICORN JOKES!

What's a unicorn's favourite hair style?
A pony tail.

Why was the unicorn arrested?
She was the mane suspect.

What did the unicorn say when he fell over?
Help – I can't giddy up.

What do unicorns wear on their feet?
Horseshoe-nicorns.

Where do sick unicorns go?
The horse-pital.

What did the unicorn say during the midnight feast?
Hoofinished the cookies?

Would you rather have a unicorn's **beard** . . .

OR clip-cloppy hooves?

The white unicorns woven into huge medieval tapestries had wispy beards and cloven hooves (hooves with two toes) – like goats, not horses!

Would you rather be a feathery unichicken ...

OR a unicow?

Two-thousand-year-old stone carvings, from the area that is now Pakistan and northwest India, show a beast with a single curved horn. But this ancient unicorn looks more like a cow than a horse!

Would you rather have a magical unicorn friend who can turn **puddles into bubble baths . . .**

OR turn **water** into **hot chocolate?**

In medieval times, people believed alicorns (unicorn horns) could purify water. Kings and queens sipped from alicorn cups to cleanse their drink of any poison. (The cups were actually carved from elephant or walrus tusks!)

Would you rather replace a unicorn's horn with . . .

a carrot,

a hot dog,

an ice-cream cone,

OR a corn-on-the-cob?

Would you rather replace a unicorn's tail with...

a broom,

a snake,

a bunch of flowers,

OR a bunny's tail?

Would you rather bring **unicorns** OR **dinosaurs to life?**

Elasmotherium was a huge animal a bit like a unicorn! This prehistoric rhinoceros was at least 1m longer and 1 tonne heavier than today's rhinos!

An old 16th-century book describes the Camphurcii, an island-dwelling unicorn with a 1m-long horn. It was said to have the front legs of a deer but the back legs of a goose – perfect for swimming after its fishy supper!

Would you rather have a **deer's** delicate cloven feet . . .

OR the **webbed feet** of a **goose?**

Would you rather have
a **pet giant squid** . . .

OR a pet narwhal with a long, unicorny horn?

Some narwhals have two horns!
These long tusks are actually teeth,
which can grow up to 3m long.

Would you rather wear **pants** knitted from a **unicorn's mane** . .

OR a wig made from a **unicorn's tail?**

Would you rather play in a unicorn football team . . .

OR go surfing with a mermaid?

FOODICORN JOKES!

What's a unicorn's favourite food?
Baked pony-tato an[d]
tuni-corn mayo.

Have you met the vegetarian unicorn?
I've not met herbivore.

What is the difference between a carrot and a unicorn?
One is a bunny feast and the other is a funny beast.

What do unicorns have for breakfast?
Uni-cornflakes.

Which unicorn helps you eat cereal?
The spoon-icorn.

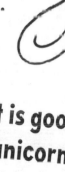

What is good advice at a unicorn picnic?
Don't bite off more than unicorn chew.

Would you rather ride with a herd of **woodland unicorns . . .**

OR join a train of **desert unicorns?**

The Karkadann, or 'Lord of the Desert', was a fearsome unicorn from old north African, Indian and Persian stories. It fought elephants and could be calmed only by the song of a dove.

Would you rather ride a unicorn to **the Moon** . . .

OR a narwhal to **the bottom of the ocean?**

In 1835, a New York newspaper falsely reported that an astronomer had seen bluish, goaty unicorns on the Moon – alongside tailless beavers and winged human-like 'man-bats'!

Would you rather eat **popcorn** with a unicorn at the **cinema** . . .

OR eat candyfloss with a unicorn at the funfair?

Would you rather be the first person to spot . . .

Scotland's **Loch Ness Monster**,

OR a real-life **unicorn?**

The unicorn is Scotland's national animal, symbolising purity and strength.

Would you rather have a **picnic** with a **unicorn** ...

OR go to the **beach** with a **mermaid?**

Would you rather tickle a **grumpy unicorn . . .**

OR pat a **sleepy dragon?**

Would you rather have a **pet unicorn**... **OR a billion dollars?**

In the business world, new companies worth more than 1 billion US dollars are called unicorns – because they're incredibly rare!

Would you rather have a unicorn as a **science** teacher . . .

OR a PE teacher?

What is a unicorn's favourite subject?
Horsetory.

What do unicorns like to play in PE?
Stable tennis.

How did the unicorn feel when the PE teacher told him to stop heading the ball?
Deflated.

What is a unicorn's favourite thing about school?
The uni-form.

What did the teacher say to the naughty unicorn?
Stop horsing around.

Would you rather **holiday** in the icy **Arctic** with a **narwhal** . . .

OR go on an **African** safari with a **unicorn?**

The mythical Ndzoodzoo from southern Africa was rumoured to have a single horn, up to 80cm long.

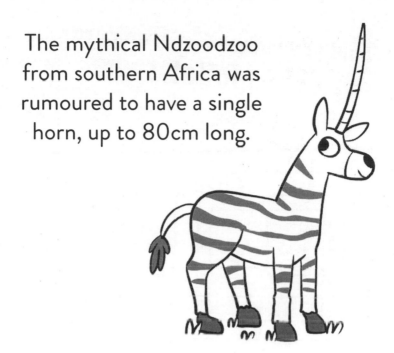

When the ferocious beast slept, its horn curled up like an elephant's trunk!

Would you rather find a unicorn on your **toilet** . . .

OR in your **bath?**

Would you rather spend a whole day **neighing** at the top of your voice . . .

OR drawing unicorn pictures **non-stop?**

Would you rather unicorns had spotty fur like a leopard . . .

OR colourful feathers like a peacock?

Would you rather all your clothes were **covered in unicorns** . . .

OR all your teddies turned into mini unicorns?

Suzy Bralliar of the USA is a record-breaking collector of unicorn stuff. In 2005, she had 2,719 items!

Would you rather ride a clean unicorn that **smells of farts . . .**

OR a muddy unicorn that **smells of roses?**

Would you rather be a unicorn seahorse OR a unicornfish?

The male unicornfish has oceans of style. It can change the colour of the bony horn on its forehead!

Would you rather have
a **sword fight** . . .

Would you rather **climb up a mountain** with a **unicorn** . . .

RAINBOW JOKES!

Did you hear about the unicorn who dyed its hair multicoloured?
It was a mane-bow.

What do unicorns wear to dinner parties?
Rainbow-ties.

**Which rainbow takes
unicorns on holiday?**
The trainbow.

**What do unicorns say when
they smell a rainbow?**
Hoofarted?

**Why were the unicorns
multicoloured and dripping wet?**
It was pouring with rainbow.

Would you rather be a knight in shining armour who **rides on a unicorn** . . .

OR a king or queen with a **stable full of unicorns?**

From 1671 to 1840, seven kings of Denmark were crowned while sitting on a brilliant white throne made with unicorn horns. (The spiralling columns and legs were really narwhal tusks!)

Would you rather **clean out** a unicorn's ear wax . . .

OR pick a unicorn's nose?